With love to our little angel, Zach
~ Mimi

THE WISE ANIMAL HANDBOOK

Kate B. Jerome

ARCADIA KIDS

Attempt new **skills** from **time** to **time.**

Just **try** to think them **through.**

And if you find you're left behind...

...then change your point of view.

Try not to **think** of just yourself.

Invent new ways to **share.**

Stay close to friends whom you can trust.

But
always
be
aware.

Avoid the tattle in the tale.

Insist that **truth** is **best.**

Embrace with pride the strengths you have.

Demand
to be
impressed.

Enjoy the peace that nature brings.

Ignore what's just for show.

Join forces when the road gets rough.

Admit
when you
don't know.

Remember **family** is the **best.**

Despite the **ups** and **downs.**

Don't **hide** from things
that you must **face.**

Make
joyful
laughing
sounds.

Eat **healthy** food to **grow** up **strong.**

Be **patient** with your **friends.**

Try not to take a stubborn stand.

Be
quick
to make
amends.

Εxcuse
yourself
when
manners
slip.

Be helpful every day.

Keep trying even when it's hard.

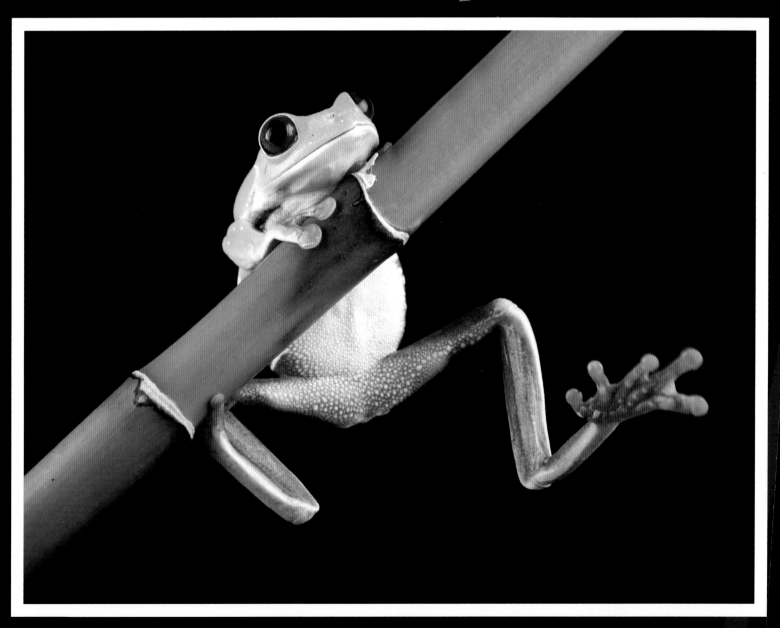

But
don't
forget to
play!

And
sing

...and **dance** each **day!**

Written by Kate B. Jerome
Design and Production: Lumina Datamatics, Inc.
Coloring Illustrations: Tom Pounders
Research: Eric Nyquist

Cover Images: See back cover

Interior Images: 002 Anetapics/Shutterstock.com; 003 George Green/Shutterstock.com; 004 Sergey Uryadnikov/Shutterstock.com; 005 Gnomeandi/Shutterstock.com; 006 Bruce MacQueen/Shutterstock.com; 007 Henk Bentlage/Shutterstock.com; 008 M.M./Shutterstock.com; 009 Mikael Damkier/Shutterstock.com; 010 Brendan van Son/Shutterstock.com; 011 Michael Pettigrew/Shutterstock.com; 012 StevenRussellSmithPhotos/Shutterstock.com; 013 Pakhnyushchy/Shutterstock.com; 014 Patjo/Shutterstock.com; 015 Quinn Martin/Shutterstock.com; 016 Lincoln Rogers/Shutterstock.com; 017 Dirk Ercken/Shutterstock.com; 018 Karel Gallas/Shutterstock.com; 019 Orangecrush/Shutterstock.com; 020 Guenter-foto/Shutterstock.com; 021 Janecat/Shutterstock.com; 022 Shironina/Shutterstock.com; 023 Annette Shaff/Shutterstock.com; 024 Vitaly Titov/Shutterstock.com; 025 Rohappy/Shutterstock.com; 026 MattiaATH/Shutterstock.com; 027 Otsphoto/Shutterstock.com; 028 FikMik/Shutterstock.com; 029 Four Oaks/Shutterstock.com; 030 Ekaterina Kolomeets/Shutterstock.com; 031 Hugh Lansdown/Shutterstock.com.

Published by Arcadia Kids, a division of Arcadia Publishing and
The History Press, Charleston, SC

For all general information contact Arcadia Publishing at:
Telephone: 843-853-2070
Email: sales@arcadiapublishing.com

For Customer Service and Orders:
Toll Free: 1-888-313-2665
Visit us on the Internet at www.arcadiapublishing.com

Library of Congress Cataloging-in-Publication data is on file with the publisher.

Printed in China

Wisconsin State **Animal**

Badger

Read Together

The badger was named the state animal in 1957. The badger can also be found on the Wisconsin state seal and the state flag!

© Kate B. Jerome 2017

Wisconsin State **Bird**

American Robin

Read Together

In 1926 and 1927, schoolchildren from all over Wisconsin voted the robin as their top choice for state bird. However, it wasn't until 1949 that the robin was actually named the state bird.

Wisconsin State Wildlife Animal

White-tailed Deer

© Kate B. Jerome 2017

Read Together

Lawmakers couldn't decide whether the badger or the white-tailed deer should be the state animal. So in 1957, they chose both! The badger became the state animal, and the white-tailed deer became the state wildlife animal.

Wisconsin State Insect

Honeybee

Read Together

A third grade class at Holy Family School in Marinette was behind the naming of the honeybee as the state insect in 1977.